Brian Turner

Grills and Barbecues

BRIAN TURNER

Grills and Barbecues

Photography by Philip Wilkins

WEIDENFELD & NICOLSON

Brian Turner

Brian Turner, chef-patron of the highly regarded Turner's in Walton Street, Knightsbridge, is one of Britain's best-known chefs. His quick and easy wit, coupled with his good-humoured Yorkshire directness, has made him a natural presenter of television and radio programmes. He is the resident chef with a weekly feature on Granada TV's *This Morning*, he has his own series on Anglia TV called *Out to Lunch with Brian Turner*, and he makes regular appearances on the BBC's popular cookery challenge *Ready Steady Cook*. He has also appeared in the *Food and Drink* series. In addition he is a frequent contributor to London Talk radio, LBC, Radio Four and regional radio programmes.

Brian trained at some of the most prestigious hotels in London and Switzerland, and ran the kitchens of the Capital Hotel to great acclaim. He opened his own restaurant, Turner's, in 1986, and is often invited to appear as 'guest chef' at leading hotels around the world. He is also Chairman of the Académie Culinaire de France, the professional body of chefs.

Contents

THE BASICS

Give me a platter of choice finnan haddie, freshly cooked in its bath of water and milk, add melted butter, a slice or two of hot toast, a pot of steaming Darjeeling tea, and you may tell the butler to dispense with the caviar, truffles, and nightingales' tongues.

CRAIG CLAIBORNE

Introduction

From my earliest days in college, I have always believed that the simplest methods of cooking – grilling, barbecuing and roasting – should be reserved for first-class cuts of meat, that is to say cuts from the parts of the animal that do not move or bend. The structure of meat is such that if a muscle is designed to move it will result in a tougher joint or cut and one that therefore requires longer, slower cooking. With modern barbecues it is not impossible to slow down the cooking process by moving the meat to the side of the barbecue, but it can be difficult to time it accurately. It is far better to start with a smaller, more tender piece of meat that will cook quickly. Beef fillet, sirloin steak, rump steak, lamb chops and cutlets are all ideal. All cuts of chicken, duck and turkey also work well on a barbecue or under a hot grill.

Fish is particularly suited to these quick cooking methods, whether it is on or off the bone. Firm-fleshed fish such as monkfish, prawns and lobster are the easiest to handle, while softer-fleshed fish are best barbecued whole. There is no doubt that whole sea bass, its cavity filled with fennel twigs, barbecued outside in the south of France makes most people think that they will never want to cook in any other way.

Some of the recipes I have chosen show how to use a marinade to provide extra flavour, while others are very simply grilled. Pitta bread, rice and lentils complement the flavours of grilled and barbecued food extremely well.

SPICED MACKEREL FILLETS
on a plum tomato salad

SERVES 4

4 mackerel, filleted and scaled
vegetable oil for brushing
1 teaspoon each of garlic salt,
  onion salt, oregano
  and paprika

Plum tomato salad

125 ml/4 fl oz olive oil
1 teaspoon creamed horseradish
1 teaspoon white wine vinegar
salt and pepper
225 g/8 oz plum tomatoes
small cos or romaine lettuce

Heat the grill or barbecue (pages 34–35).

To make the salad dressing, whisk together the oil, horseradish, vinegar and salt and pepper to taste.

Run your fingers over the flesh of the mackerel to make sure no bones remain; use tweezers to pull out any tiny bones. Cut each fillet in half. Brush the fish with a little oil and then pass the flesh side through the spices. Place the fish, spice side down, on the grill. Cook for 2–3 minutes – do not overcook – then turn and cook the other side.

Slice the tomatoes and lay on four plates. Shred the lettuce and toss in some of the dressing. Put the lettuce on top of the tomatoes. Lay the barbecued fish on top and sprinkle with the dressing. Serve at once.

Serve with a warm potato salad and mustard mayonnaise, and finish with a lemon tart and clotted cream.

BARBECUED CORN ON THE COB
with cucumber relish

SERVES 4

4 corn on the cob

Cucumber relish

1 cucumber
450 g/1 lb green tomatoes
2 onions
1 red pepper
salt
600 ml/1 pint white vinegar
225 g/8 oz brown sugar
225 g/8 oz white sugar
1 tablespoon plain flour
1 tablespoon curry powder
1 teaspoon mustard powder

First make the cucumber relish. Slice the cucumber in half lengthways, scoop out the seeds and cut off the ends. Finely chop the cucumber, tomatoes, onions and red pepper. Place in a colander, sprinkle with salt and leave overnight.

The next day, pour off any liquid that has drained out and put the vegetables into a preserving pan together with the vinegar and both sugars. Boil for 1 hour.

Mix the flour, curry powder and mustard with a splash of vinegar to make a paste. Stir into the pan and simmer for 30 minutes.

There are two ways of barbecuing the corn cobs. You could trim off the husks and silks, then boil the cobs in salted water for 15 minutes; drain, refresh in cold water and brown them on the barbecue for about 5 minutes. Alternatively, you could pull down the husks, trim off the silks and soak the cobs in water for about 5 minutes. Then pull the husks back up and twist to seal. Grill on a hot barbecue for 15–20 minutes.

Serve the corn hot from the grill, accompanied by the cucumber relish.

This is a great dish to serve with the spit-roasted chicken with lemon and lemon balm (page 22), and then perhaps enjoy a white chocolate mousse.

KEBABS OF TIGER PRAWNS
with a roasted tomato and mint salsa

SERVES 4

12 uncooked tiger prawns,
    shelled
2 tablespoons olive oil
1 garlic clove, finely chopped

Roasted tomato and mint salsa
3 beefsteak tomatoes
1 garlic clove, finely chopped
juice of ½ lime
1 chilli, finely chopped, including
    its seeds
1 tablespoon finely chopped
    fresh coriander
2 tablespoons finely chopped
    fresh mint
½ teaspoon grated lime zest
½ teaspoon grated orange zest
salt and pepper

To serve
boiled new potatoes or
    potato salad

Heat the grill or barbecue (pages 34–35). If using wooden skewers, soak them in cold water for about 30 minutes.

Slit the prawns along their backs and pull out the dark vein, opening them out butterfly style. Place them in a shallow dish with the oil and garlic and leave to marinate for 30 minutes.

To make the salsa, sear the tomatoes under a very hot grill or over a flame until their skins blacken and blister. Chop finely while they are still warm. Mix with all the other ingredients and leave to cool.

Fix the prawns on the skewers and grill until they turn pink, turning once. Serve the prawns on a bed of potatoes, with the salsa spooned around.

I often have these prawns with a green salad. Beforehand, I love a spicy gazpacho soup, and afterwards some bread and soft cheeses such as goats' cheese or feta.

BARBECUED TROUT
with spinach and bacon

SERVES 4

70 g/2½ oz unsalted butter
1 large onion, finely chopped
225 g/8 oz baby spinach,
  washed and roughly chopped
salt and pepper
4 trout, gutted and cleaned
8 rashers of smoked
  streaky bacon

Red wine sauce
1 teaspoon vegetable oil
125 g/4 oz streaky bacon, cut
  into small strips (lardons)
125 g/4 oz mushrooms, sliced
150 ml/5 fl oz red wine

Heat the grill or barbecue (pages 34–35).

Melt 50 g/2 oz of the butter in a large saucepan, add the onion and cook over a medium heat until softened, about 5 minutes. Add the spinach and cook briefly until the spinach wilts. Leave until cool enough to handle.

Season the spinach and onion mixture with salt and plenty of pepper, then use to fill the four trout. Wrap two rashers of bacon around each trout and secure with a cocktail stick. Grill the trout for 8–10 minutes, turning once, until crisp on the outside and tender in the middle.

Meanwhile, make the sauce. Heat the oil in a saucepan, add the bacon lardons and cook for 5–6 minutes, then add the mushrooms and stir over medium heat for about 2 minutes. Pour in the red wine, bring to the boil, then reduce the heat and simmer for 5 minutes. At the last minute, stir in the remaining 15 g/½ oz butter to give a glossy finish.

Serve the trout on warmed plates, with the red wine sauce poured around.

Why not try sautéed potatoes with the trout, and perhaps a light prawn salad to start?

GRILLED SALMON
with cucumber salad

SERVES 4

4 salmon steaks, about 175 g/
    6 oz each, scaled
1 garlic clove, finely chopped
bunch of coriander,
    finely chopped
1 tablespoon mustard
1 tablespoon tomato ketchup
1 teaspoon Tabasco sauce
1 tablespoon white wine vinegar
1 teaspoon sugar
salt and pepper
150 ml/5 fl oz olive oil

Cucumber salad

2 cucumbers
salt and pepper
1 teaspoon chopped fresh mint
2 tablespoons yogurt

Leave the skin on the salmon and place in a shallow dish. Mix the garlic and coriander with the mustard, ketchup, Tabasco, vinegar, sugar and salt and pepper. Gradually stir in the oil. Pour the marinade over the salmon and leave in the refrigerator for 24 hours.

Peel the cucumbers, slice thinly, place in a colander and sprinkle with salt. Leave to stand for 1 hour.

Heat the grill or barbecue (pages 34–35).

Squeeze out the liquid that has drained from the cucumbers, add pepper to taste and mix with the chopped mint. Stir in the yogurt. Grill the salmon until cooked to your liking, brushing with the marinade as it cooks. Serve hot, with new potatoes and the cucumber salad.

Smoked haddock rillettes with toast is a great starter before this salmon dish. The perfect pudding would be strawberries and clotted cream.

KEBABS OF CURRIED TURKEY
with banana salsa

SERVES 4

450 g/1 lb turkey
1 teaspoon corn oil
2 tablespoons curry powder

Banana salsa
2 ripe bananas
1 teaspoon finely chopped
    red chilli
1 tablespoon fresh lime juice
1 tablespoon chopped
    fresh coriander
½ red pepper, diced

To serve
boiled rice or rice salad

Cut the turkey into 4 cm/1½ inch chunks. Mix the oil and curry powder together in a bowl, add the turkey and turn to coat in the mixture. Leave to marinate for about 30 minutes at room temperature or up to 4 hours in the refrigerator.

To make the salsa, dice the bananas and mix with all the remaining ingredients. Chill well.

Heat the grill or barbecue (pages 34–35). If using wooden skewers, soak them in cold water for about 30 minutes.

Fix the turkey pieces on the skewers and grill for about 10 minutes or until cooked through but not dried out, turning regularly. Serve on a bed of rice, with the banana salsa on the side.

Start with smoked salmon and brown bread; fresh pineapple makes a refreshing dessert.

SPIT-ROASTED CHICKEN
with lemon and lemon balm

SERVES 4

1 roasting chicken
sprigs of lemon balm
150 ml/5 fl oz olive oil
pinch of paprika
pinch of cayenne
pinch of salt
juice of ½ lemon

Lemon confit
2 lemons
50 g/2 oz sugar

For the lemon confit, slice the lemons into thin rounds. Blanch in boiling water for 1 minute and refresh under cold running water. Put the sugar in a saucepan with 150 ml/5 fl oz water, add the lemon slices and simmer for 10 minutes. Leave to cool.

Remove the wishbone from the chicken and loosen the skin. Spread the lemon confit and lemon balm under the skin and on the breast and legs. Mix together the oil, paprika, cayenne and salt. Roast the chicken on a spit for about 40 minutes, brushing frequently with the oil mixture.

Alternatively, if you do not have a roasting spit, cook the chicken in a hot oven (200°C/400°F/Gas Mark 6) for 30–40 minutes, then finish cooking on the barbecue, to give it a delicious smoky flavour.

Serve hot, with lemon juice squeezed over.

As an accompaniment, serve coleslaw and potatoes baked in their jackets. Alternatively, serve with couscous, grilled aubergines and a green salad. Follow with apple tart and custard.

LAMB STEAKS IN MINT OIL
with rice

SERVES 4

4 lamb chump chops,
   about 175 g/6 oz each
½ bunch of mint, chopped
½ bunch of parsley, chopped
125 ml/4 fl oz groundnut oil
1 teaspoon olive oil
½ onion, chopped
175 g/6 oz basmati rice
1 teaspoon turmeric
salt and pepper
15 g/½ oz butter

Heat the grill or barbecue (pages 34–35). Preheat the oven to 200°C/400°F/Gas Mark 6.

Trim the lamb chops of excess fat and place in a shallow dish. Put the mint and parsley in a food processor and blend, gradually adding the groundnut oil. Pour over the lamb and leave to marinate for about 5 minutes, while you prepare the rice.

Heat the olive oil in a casserole, add the onion and cook over a low heat until softened. Add the rice and one and a half times its volume of water, stir and bring to the boil. Add the turmeric. Cover with greased greaseproof paper and bake in the oven for 15 minutes or until the rice is tender. Season to taste and stir in the butter.

Grill the lamb for about 3 minutes on each side; it should still be pink in the middle. Brush with the mint oil, season and leave to rest for 10 minutes. Serve on the rice.

To make this the most perfect meal, start with a simple asparagus salad with Parmesan cheese and freshly ground black pepper. Follow with coffee crème brûlée and vanilla ice cream.

BEEF RIB STEAK
with a mustard and shallot topping

SERVES 4

25 g/1 oz unsalted butter
325 g/12 oz shallots, chopped
1 garlic clove, chopped
1 tablespoon white wine vinegar
1 tablespoon Dijon mustard
1 tablespoon chopped fresh
   coriander
salt and pepper
2 beef rib steaks on the bone,
   about 675 g/1½ lb each
vegetable oil for brushing

Heat the grill or barbecue (pages 34–35).

Heat the butter in a saucepan, add the shallots and cook over a low heat until softened. Add the garlic and cook slowly for 20 minutes. Add the vinegar and cook until reduced to a dry consistency. Stir in the mustard and coriander and season to taste.

Brush the steaks with oil and grill, turning regularly, until cooked rare. Cut the beef off the bone, slice and serve hot, covered with the shallot mixture.

Whenever I think of this dish I think of garlic roast potatoes and green beans. First I might serve hot grilled prawns or a prawn salad, with a lemon posset and raspberries to finish.

Honey-glazed pork chops

SERVES 4

4 tablespoons lemon juice
2 tablespoons clear honey
salt and pepper
4 pork chops, about 175 g/
   6 oz each
chopped fresh sage

Heat the grill or barbecue (pages 34−35).

Mix together the lemon juice, honey, salt and pepper.
Brush the pork chops with the mixture and leave to
stand for 15−20 minutes.

Grill the chops over high heat for 4−5 minutes. Turn
down the heat or raise the barbecue grid and continue
to cook for a further 5 minutes. Turn the chops over,
taking care not to pierce the meat, and turn the heat up
once again. After a few minutes turn down the heat and
finish cooking. Season with salt and sprinkle some sage
over the chops. Serve at once.

Before the pork chops try a tomato and onion salad. Serve
noodles with the chops, and finish the meal with a fruit tart
and ice cream.

Butterflied leg of lamb

SERVES 6–8

2 kg/4½ lb leg of lamb, boned*
3 large garlic cloves
2 sprigs of rosemary
3–4 tablespoons olive oil
salt and pepper

* Ask your butcher to take out the bone in one cut, so the lamb can be opened out flat.

Lay the lamb lay out flat. Make 12 incisions in the lamb using the tip of a sharp knife. Slice each of the garlic cloves into four pieces and break the rosemary into 12 smaller sprigs. Place a slice of garlic and a rosemary sprig into each of the incisions in the lamb. Leave to marinate for 4 hours at room temperature or overnight in the refrigerator.

Heat the grill or barbecue (pages 34–35).

Brush the lamb with olive oil and season well. Grill for 12–20 minutes on each side; cooking time will depend partly on the heat of the grill, partly on how well done you like your lamb. Should the lamb blacken too quickly, raise the barbecue grid slightly or turn down the heat. Leave the lamb to rest for 10 minutes before slicing. Serve hot.

For an ideal menu, serve fresh mint sauce and new potatoes with this dish, and finish with a tarte tatin.

BAKED BANANAS IN RUM

SERVES 4

4 bananas
2 tablespoons brown sugar
grated zest of 2 oranges
2 tablespoons dark rum
25 g/1 oz butter

To serve
clotted cream

Heat the barbecue (page 35) or preheat the oven to 180°C/350°F/Gas Mark 4.

Cut each banana into three. Mix the sugar and orange zest with a splash of rum, then mix with the bananas.

Butter a rectangle of foil, about 40 x 30 cm/16 x 12 inches. Fold it in half and seal two of the three edges. Pour in the banana mixture and add the extra rum. Seal and put on the barbecue or bake in the oven for 5 minutes. Serve hot, with clotted cream.

A simple pudding for any occasion. The beef with a mustard and shallot topping (page 26) would be particularly good before these bananas.

The Basics

GRILLING

In the past few years, chargrilling has become an extremely fashionable cooking process, imitating the intense heat and distinctive blackened stripes of the barbecue. It can be done in a ridged chargrilling or griddle pan or directly under a hot grill.

If you want to buy a ridged pan, choose a heavy iron one that will withstand the very high temperatures. For cooking under the grill you will need a heavy baking sheet that will not buckle with direct heat.

Before you start to cook the food, heat the chargrilling pan on the hob or under the grill. Alternatively line the baking sheet with foil and place under the grill to heat. When thoroughly hot, brush the pan with oil and add the food - it should sizzle when it hits the pan. (The exception to this rule is duck breast, which can be placed skin-side down on the cold ridged pan and brought up to cooking temperature: this draws out the fat from under the skin.)

Unless the recipe says otherwise, resist the temptation to move food around while it cooks. Too much movement releases juices and 'steams' the food – with this cooking method you want to keep the juices sealed in. Don't overcrowd the pan, or the heat will be dispersed. Cook in batches if necessary. Turn food quickly, using tongs, so that it doesn't lose heat.

BARBECUING

There are many different kinds of barbecue on the market today; the one you choose may be decided by cost, but as far as I am concerned a real barbecue is over charcoal – charcoal lumps and briquettes are widely available. Tongs are the most important piece of equipment, so you can turn the food and remove it without losing it between the bars.

One of the most difficult aspects of barbecuing is getting it correctly and evenly lit. Use a barbecue lighter and never paraffin or petrol: they are dangerous and will taint the food with their smell. When the barbecue is lit it should be left alone for the heat to be evenly distributed. The flames will eventually die down and the charcoal will look as if it is covered with a white ash. This is the time to commence cooking.

Before you put the food on the barbecue, brush the bars with oil to prevent the food from sticking.

Food has to be cooked at the right distance from the heat to allow the food to cook through without the outside becoming too black. Remember, though, that for a lot of people some amount of blackening is an essential part of the taste of barbecued food.

MARINADES

The simplicity of grilled or barbecued food is one of the most attractive features of these styles of cooking. Vegetables, fish and first-class cuts of meat taste wonderful charred from the grill or permeated with a faint smoky flavour. However, barbecuing and grilling also lend themselves to the additional flavours of marinades.

Oils baste the food as it cooks; vinegar, wine or lemon juice can be used to tenderize the slightly tougher cuts of meat; herbs and spices add extra flavour; and most marinades can be made into a complementary sauce.

The food can usually be marinated and kept in the refrigerator up to a day ahead, but some fruits – for example pineapples and papayas – contain enzymes that can break meat down too much.

GRILLED VEGETABLES

Grilled and barbecued vegetables add colour, texture and nutritional value by way of accompaniment; they are also very easy to do. Natural sugars in the vegetables caramelize to create a delicious flavour, which combines beautifully with the smoky aroma of the barbecue.

Besides corn on the cob (page 12), there are a number of other vegetables that lend themselves to this style of cooking. Most of them can be simply brushed with oil just before grilling.

Aubergines and courgettes should be sliced, either crossways or lengthways, about 5 mm/¼ inch thick.

Fennel should be sliced downwards, about 5 mm/¼ inch thick. Carefully trim off any woody parts at the base and top.

Mushrooms Choose large, open, flat mushrooms and grill open-side down first. Button mushrooms should be threaded on to a wooden skewer, which you have first soaked in water for about 30 minutes so it doesn't burn.

Onions Cut small or medium onions into quarters. Spring onions are also delicious grilled.

Peppers should be sliced downwards into quarters.

Tomatoes Small tomatoes should be cooked whole, in their skins. Large, firm beefsteak tomatoes should be sliced about 2 cm/¾ inch thick.

Classic Cooking

STARTERS

Lesley Waters A former chef and now a popular television cook, appearing regularly on *Ready Steady Cook* and *Can't Cook Won't Cook*. Author of several cookery books.

VEGETABLE SOUPS

Elisabeth Luard Cookery writer for the *Sunday Telegraph Magazine* and author of *European Peasant Food* and *European Festival Food*, which won a Glenfiddich Award.

GOURMET SALADS

Sonia Stevenson The first woman chef in the UK to be awarded a Michelin star, at the Horn of Plenty in Devon. Author of *The Magic of Saucery* and *Fresh Ways with Fish*.

FISH AND SHELLFISH

Gordon Ramsay Chef/proprietor of London's Aubergine restaurant, recently awarded its second Michelin star, and author of Glenfiddich Award-winning *A Passion for Flavour*.

CHICKEN, DUCK AND GAME

Nick Nairn Chef/patron of Braeval restaurant near Aberfoyle in Scotland, whose BBC-TV series *Wild Harvest* was last summer's most successful cookery series, accompanied by a book.

LIVERS, SWEETBREADS AND KIDNEYS

Simon Hopkinson Former chef/patron at London's Bibendum restaurant, columnist and author of *Roast Chicken and Other Stories* and *The Prawn Cocktail Years*.

VEGETARIAN

Rosamond Richardson Author of several vegetarian titles, including *The Great Green Cookbook* and *Food from Green Places*.

PASTA

Joy Davies One of the creators of *BBC Good Food Magazine*, she has been food editor of *She, Woman* and *Options* and written for the *Guardian, Daily Telegraph* and *Harpers & Queen*.

CHEESE DISHES

Rose Elliot The UK's most successful vegetarian cookery writer and author of many books, including *Not Just a Load of Old Lentils* and *The Classic Vegetarian Cookbook*.

POTATO DISHES

Patrick McDonald Former chef/patron of the acclaimed Epicurean restaurant in Cheltenham, and food consultant to Sir Rocco Forte Hotels.

BISTRO

Anne Willan Founder and director of La Varenne Cookery School in Burgundy and West Virginia. Author of many books and a specialist in French cuisine.

ITALIAN

Anna Del Conte Author of several books on Italian food, including *The Gastronomy of Italy, Secrets from an Italian Kitchen* and *The Classic Food of Northern Italy* (chosen as the 1996 Guild of Food Writers Book of the Year).

Vietnamese

Nicole Routhier One of the United States' most popular cookery writers, her books include *Cooking Under Wraps, Nicole Routhier's Fruit Cookbook* and the award-winning *The Foods of Vietnam*.

Malaysian

Jill Dupleix One of Australia's best known cookery writers and broadcasters, with columns in the *Sydney Morning Herald* and *Elle*. Her books include *New Food* and *Allegro al dente*.

Peking Cuisine

Helen Chen Author of *Chinese Home Cooking,* she learned to cook traditional Peking dishes from her mother, Joyce Chen, the *grande dame* of Chinese cooking in the United States.

Stir-fries

Kay Fairfax A writer and broadcaster whose books include *100 Great Stir-fries, Homemade* and *The Australian Christmas Book.*

Noodles

Terry Durack Australia's most widely read restaurant critic and co-editor of the *Sydney Morning Herald Good Food Guide*. He is the author of *YUM*, a book of stories and recipes.

North Indian Curries

Pat Chapman Founded the Curry Club in 1982. A regular broadcaster on television and radio, he is the author of 20 books, which have sold more than 1 million copies.

Grills and Barbecues

Brian Turner Chef/patron of Turner's in Knightsbridge and one of Britain's most popular food broadcasters; he appears frequently on *Ready Steady Cook, Food and Drink* and many other television programmes.

Summer and Winter Casseroles

Anton Edelmann Maître Chef des Cuisines at the Savoy Hotel, London. Author of six cookery books, he has also appeared on television.

Traditional Puddings

Tessa Bramley Chef/patron of the acclaimed Old Vicarage restaurant in Ridgeway, Derbyshire and author of *The Instinctive Cook*.

Decorated Cakes

Jane Asher Author of several cookery books and a novel. She has also appeared in her own television series, *Jane Asher's Christmas* (1995).

Favourite Cakes

Mary Berry One of Britain's leading cookery writers, her numerous books include *Mary Berry's Ultimate Cake Book*. She has made many television and radio appearances.

Ice Creams and Semi Freddi

Ann and Franco Taruschio Owners of the renowned Walnut Tree Inn near Abergavenny in Wales, soon to appear in a television series, *Franco and Friends: Food from the Walnut Tree*. They have written three books together.

First published in 1997 by
George Weidenfeld & Nicolson
The Orion Publishing Group
Orion House
5 Upper St Martin's Lane
London WC2H 9EA

British Library Cataloguing-in-Publication data
A catalogue record for this book is available from
the British Library

ISBN 0 297 82338 8

Designed by Lucy Holmes
Edited by Maggie Ramsay
Food styling by Louise Pickford
Typesetting by Tiger Typeset